TEASE YOUR BRAIN,

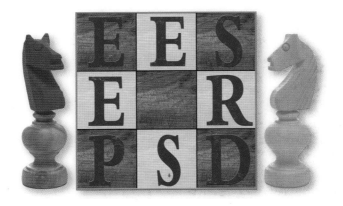

TEST YOUR SMARTS

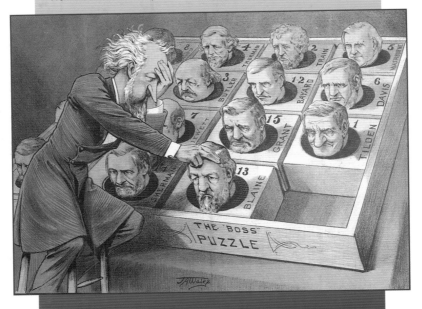

Puck magazine cartoon about the 1880 Presidential Election. From the book *The 15 Puzzle* by Jerry Slocum and Dic Sonneveld, The Slocum Puzzle Foundation, Beverly Hills, (2006) www.SlocumPuzzles.com.

From the moment it was published in 1880, The Fifteen Puzzle launched a rage.

Jack Botermans

TEASE YOUR BRAIN,

TEST YOUR SMARTS

Sterling Publishing Co., Inc.
New York

Library of Congress Cataloging-in-Publication Data Available

10 9 8 7 6 5 4 3 2 1

Published in 2007 by Sterling Publishing Co., Inc.
387 Park Avenue South, New York, NY 10016
© 2006 by Bookman International and Jack Boetermans, Netherlands
Published in the English language by arrangement with Bookman international B.V.,
Netherlands
Concept, text, design, and photography by Jack Botermans, Netherlands
Distributed in Canada by Sterling Publishing
c/o Canadian Manda Group, 165 Dufferin Street
Toronto, Ontario, Canada M6K 3H6
Distributed in the United Kingdom by GMC Distribution Services
Castle Place, 166 High Street, Lewes, East Sussex, England BN7 1XU
Distributed in Australia by Capricorn Link (Australia) Pty. Ltd.
P.O. Box 704, Windsor, NSW 2756, Australia

Printed in China

Sterling ISBN-13: 978-1-4027-3650-6
          ISBN-10: 1-4027-3650-9

For information about custom editions, special sales, premium and
corporate purchases, please contact Sterling Special Sales
Department at 800-805-5489 or specialsales@sterlingpub.com.

Instructions to the Reader

This book features every type of puzzle in the various puzzle categories. There are number crunching and algebraic puzzles, puzzles with missing images, optical illusions, mazes, and a myriad of other types of puzzles.

You can start at the beginning and work page by page, but you can also pick pages at random. Easy, medium, and difficult puzzles are mixed up. When trying to find a solution, don't give up too easily and don't look it up too quickly in the chapter "Solutions" (page 190). Instead, leave the puzzle till later and then try again. Keep the notes you made. After a while you will start recognizing certain patterns. Try and remember them and apply them to new puzzles. You'll also discover that you can make your own variations on some puzzles. Write them down and show them to friends and colleagues.

Sometimes it's necessary to make a photocopy of a puzzle and work with that. You can also buy transparent paper to cover the puzzle and copy it with a special felt-tip pen. You can wipe the transparent paper clean with a moist cloth.

Puzzling will bring you relaxation and satisfaction. It dispels boredom and helps you fight a somber mood.

BRAINTEASERS

According to official records, the first puzzle as far as we are aware dates back to the third century B.C. It was of Greek origin and was called "Ostomachion," also known as the 'Loculus Archimedes" (Archimedes' box). A cross between a jigsaw and a tangram puzzle, it consisted of 14 pieces that could be arranged to make a square. The same pieces could also be formed to create interesting figures, such as the elephant below.*

* In *The book Tangram* by Jerry Slocum, also published by Sterling, you'll find extensive documentation on this subject.

Puzzles are as diverse as life itself, and therefore an extensive genealogical tree can be made from them depending on the type. Originally devised for amusement and educational purposes, puzzles can be numerical or letter-based, or feature missing images, optical illusions, mazes, riddles, and a whole assortment of other combinations too numerous to mention.

During the course of the twentieth century it became clear that people who solved puzzles were performing a mental exercise that helped to maintain the condition of their memory. For example, Einstein frequently rested from his work researching "time in relation to space" by doing a lot of puzzles. What's more, figuring out puzzles is a fun way to spend your leisure time, and we hope this book helps you do that with pleasure. You can start from the beginning, and proceed page by page, or you can select the pages you want to do at random. Puzzles are also an interesting way to link up with other people. Other enthusiasts are always keen to swap favorites from their treasure trove of puzzles! So without further ado, let me wish you lots of fun as you journey through this book, discovering a whole paradise of puzzle pleasure.

Jack Botermans

Ink Blots

Study the ink stains. Yes, it does look like someone used a leaky pen, but continue looking until you can decipher what the person wrote.

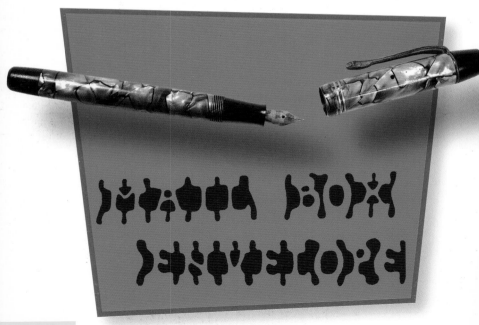

Illusion

Is the green of this bar the same shade over the whole width?

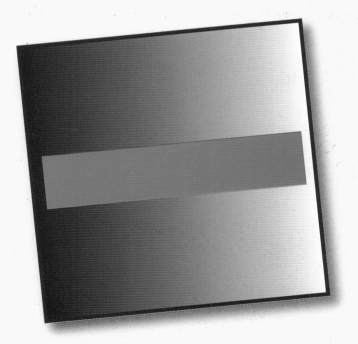

A Sharp-Witted Square ...

By cutting only one of the triangles below into two parts you can make an exact square of the whole.

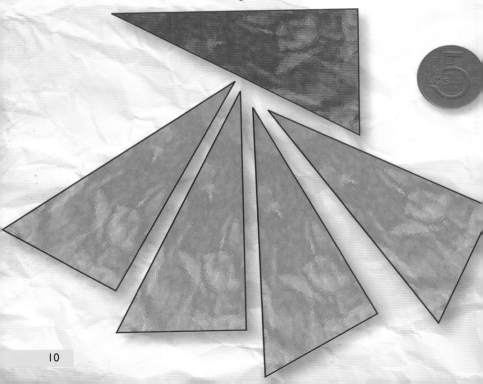

"Lay-Down" Puzzle

Lay down ten coins on the model below in such a way that as many horizontal, vertical, or diagonal rows of an even number of coins are created.

Only Three ...

Add three straight lines to this figure, to create 13 triangles.

New York

We want to take a stroll through New York. Where should we go to find a bit of nature and green in this city? They really made a mess of it on the signpost and the letters are all mixed up!

Dogs ...

What do you need to know before you start to
teach a dog something?

What's What?

Which number should replace the
question mark?

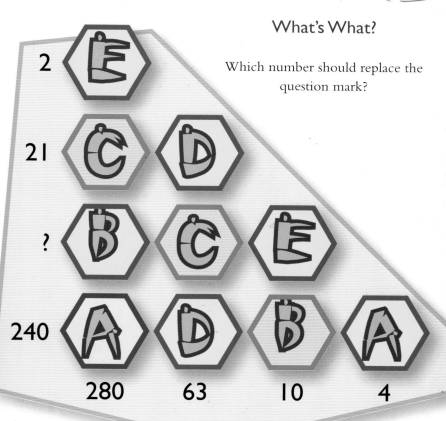

Sign Language

Just try and figure out these hands. What is being said here?

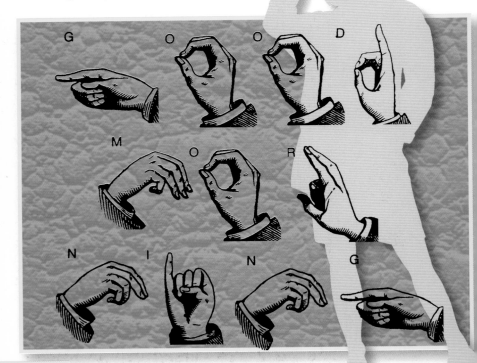

Secret Language?

Can you decode this secret message?

Logic!

Which number should replace the question mark?

Find the Animal ...

There are many unnecessary lines here. Black them out and find the hidden animal.

From the collection of Jerry Slocum, USA.

Hopscotch

A hopscotch diagram for a moment of relaxation. There's just one problem: there's a number missing. Which one should replace the question mark?

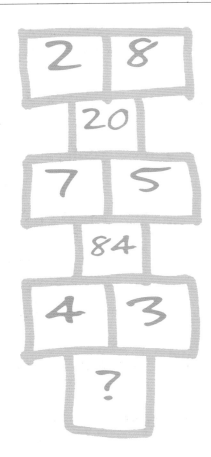

two

beer

Famous Saying?

or

The upper half of the text seems to have fallen by the wayside. Can you still figure out what it says?

not

two

beer

William

Shakebeer

Politicians Sleep the Sleep of the Dead …

There is a lot of nonsense printed in the gossip mags.
Look for yourself.
Which politicians are mentioned here?

RHOTEDOE VESOTOELR

DAREGL DOFR

SWITNON LHCCILRUH

DALOG RIME

HIRADRC XINON

Marbles

Which marble doesn't belong here?

Cut Up!

What should be the fourth symbol and which symbols should be pictured below it? There should be only four symbols in total.

A	B	C	D	E
F	G	H	I	J
K	L	M	N	O
P	Q	R	S	T
U	V	W	X	Z

Well-Known Names

Try and break the code to find three well-known names.

VI-ZI-W4-X3-UI-W4-XI

W4-UI-W3-VI-Z3

ZI-V3-V5-X2-X4

Blowing Test

How do you blow over a big, heavy book?
A nice challenge to try out among your acquaintances.

From the Collection of Jerry Slocum, USA.

Magical Matches

How do you make a quadrangular star out of four matches that have been broken in half?

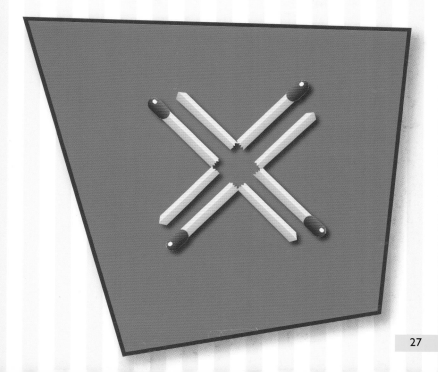

27

C W Z

Question Mark

A Q R

Which letter should replace the question mark?

? L X

Chess Puzzle

Where to begin? Find the right starting point and via knight's moves look for a word of 10 letters that begins and ends with the same letter.

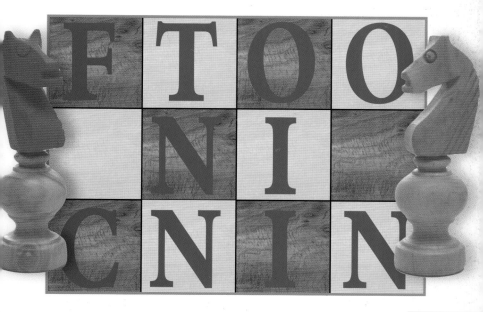

Just Out for a Sec …

Look for the undertaker.
A U.S. picture puzzle circa 1890.

There was a young man of Balquidder,
Who married (for cash) an old "widder;"
  She pulls out all his hair,
  And of cash keeps him bare,
He is tired of his life in Balquidder.

Puzzle: Find the Undertaker.

Pointed Affair ...

How many rectangles and squares can you make by connecting the 12 points below with straight lines?

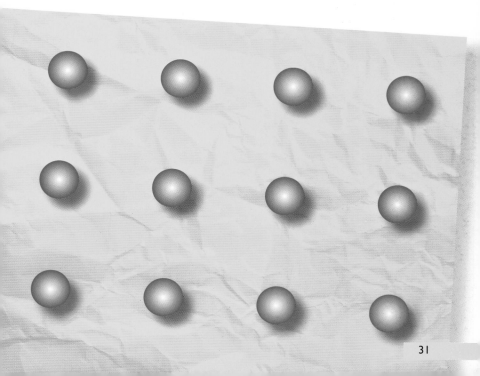

Turning This Way and That ...

By cutting this sheet of paper twice can you divide it in three pieces
and then make a perfect square?

Backward Sports?

Name three sports that are performed backward.

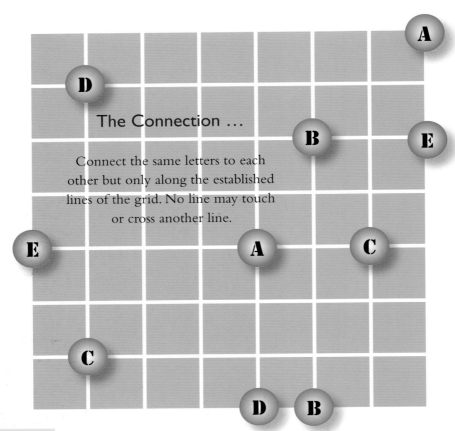

The Connection ...

Connect the same letters to each
other but only along the established
lines of the grid. No line may touch
or cross another line.

King …?

An imposing figure he was, this famed king. With the information given below, can you decipher his name?

It begins with 500 and ends with 500. The five is in the middle. The first of all the letters and the first of all the numbers have their place in between them. So, what's this king's name?

Closed Squares

Replace the letters A through J by numbers in such a way that one of the numbers 1 through 14 appears in all the enclosed spaces. But...the numbers inside each square should add up to 21.

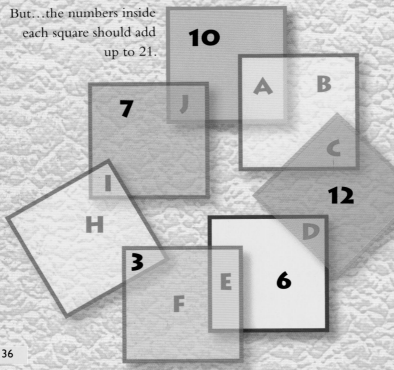

Light in the Darkness …

Which of the two yellow circles
is lighter?

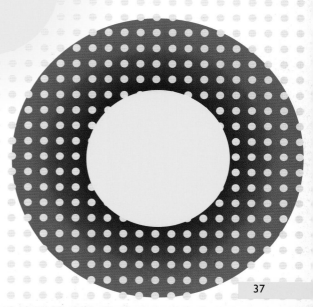

Odd One Out ...

Which of these four shapes does not belong?

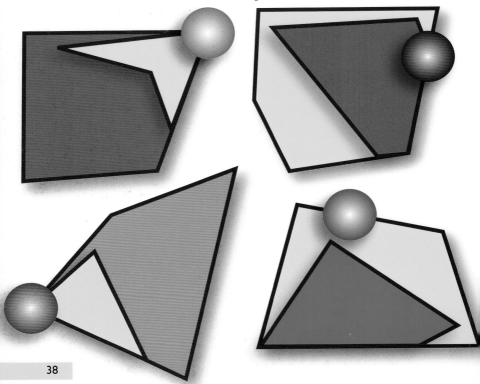

Just 15 ...

Place the numbers 1 through 15 in the squares in such a way that each pair in the dark blue spaces adds up to 15 and that each column, row and diagonal of "four" numbers adds up to 30.

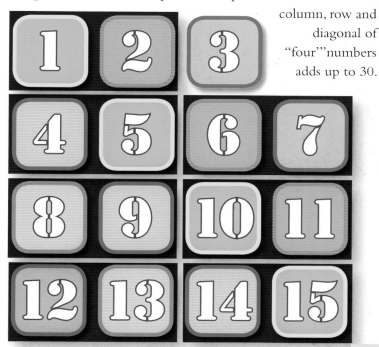

Gravity ...

Can you drop a coin and a piece of paper from a height of about 1 yard (1 m) simultaneously and make them fall on the ground simultaneously? You are not allowed to use any other objects except the coin and the piece of paper, and the paper should not be folded around the coin.

Next?

Which letter should logically replace
the question mark?

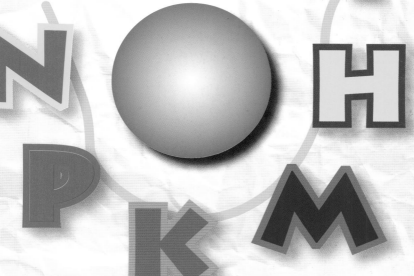

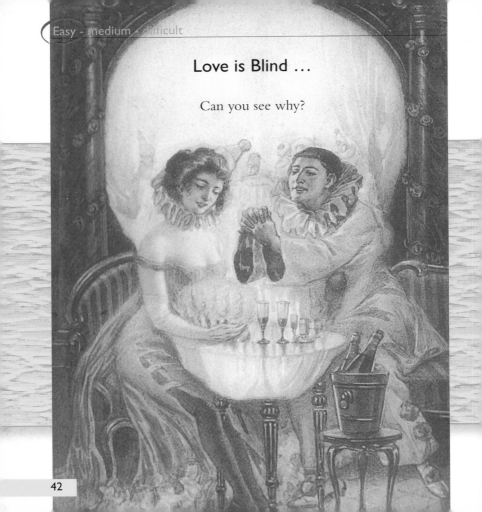

Love is Blind ...

Can you see why?

Logistic Anagrams

The letters of these names of cities have been mixed up.
Can you decipher the names?

MERDASTAM

EYORNKW

ASOLNEGESL

CANOALEBR

ADRIMD

OREM

Type Case ...

Can you find the letters belonging in the squares with the question marks?

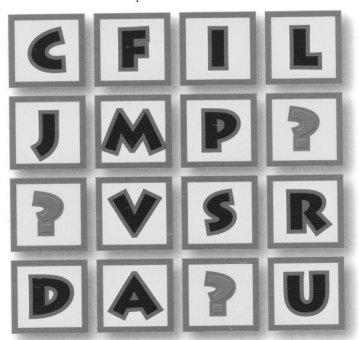

Torture

A four-digit number is divided by a two-digit number. The answer
is a four-digit number. Only three numbers are used.

Do you know which ones?

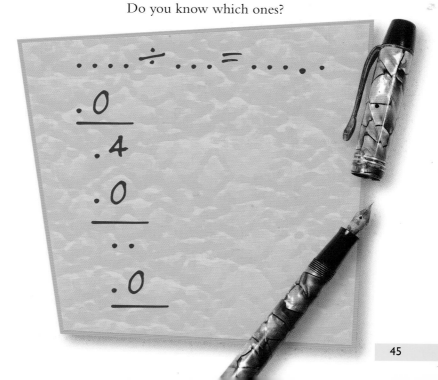

$$\cdots \div \cdots = \cdots$$

Water Running Uphill …

Place a burning candle in a bowl with water and press a glass down over the candle. As the flame dies, watch the water rise slowly inside the glass.

Logic!

Which number should replace the question mark?

That Poor Woman!

She's been busy gathering wood, but her husband doesn't help her carry it. Can you find her husband?

From the collection of Jerry Slocum, USA.

Brainteaser

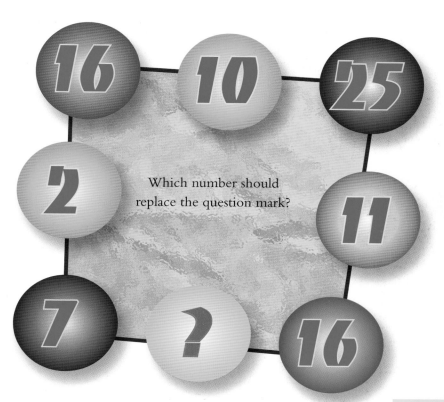

Which number should replace the question mark?

What's That For?

Sometimes you see an object that seems to serve
no purpose at all. This one is a good example.
Can you figure out what it is?

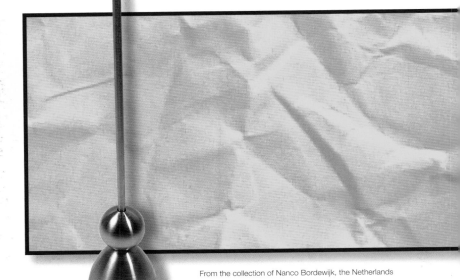

From the collection of Nanco Bordewijk, the Netherlands

Capital

Now what's this? Who has stenciled this name? And written it backward on top of that? Find the name of this European capital.

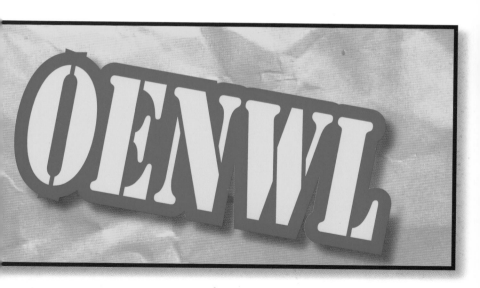

Logical Numbering

A bit of logical thinking and you'll find the number that should replace the question mark…

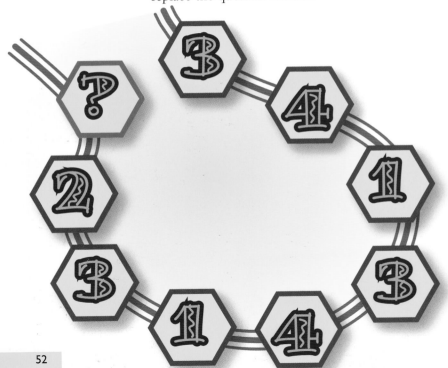

The Joke(r) Is on You …

Make a bet that you can crawl through a playing card. Don't be
afraid to up the ante, for you're going to win this bet.
But how?

15, 16, and 17...

The numbers 0 through 14 are divided over three colored shapes. Even so, the numbers 15, 16, and 17 still have to be placed in one or more of the shapes. You have the honor of figuring out where they belong.

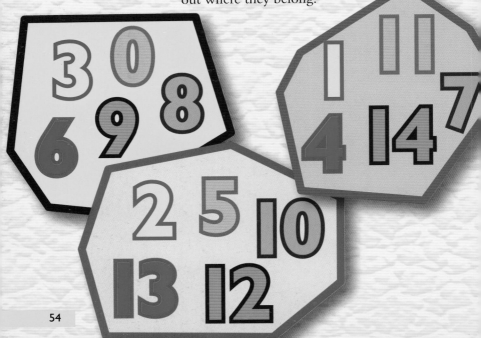

Patching Up a Quarrel …

You're in an argument with someone
who threatens to overpower you. How
do you make sure he doesn't?
1. Tell this person you will stop him
   with your mental powers.
2. Spread out a handkerchief on the
   floor.
3. Tell him to stand with his toes on
   one side of the handkerchief.
4. You stand with your toes on the
   other side of it.
The question is: how do you make
yourself invulnerable to your
opponent?

Star Puzzle

Which letter should replace the question mark?

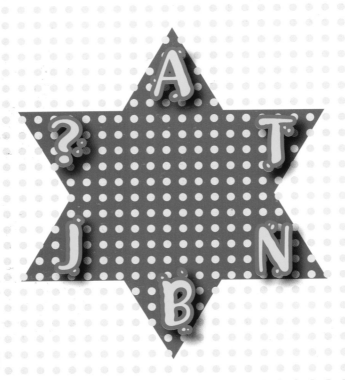

Turning This Way and That

Which figure should be number 1?

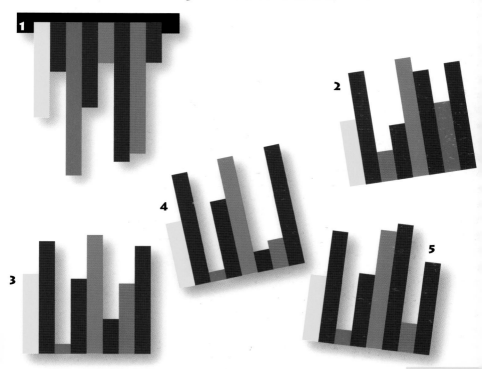

Famous Race Tracks

This horse competed on the race tracks mentioned below. On each
race track, he had a different number. Which number did he have
on his back in Hilversum?
And is he riding toward you or away from you?

ASCOT NO. 58

DUINDIGT NO. 88

CHANTILLY NO. 104

MONTE CARLO NO. 116

HILVERSUM NO. ?

58

Quite a Walk …

Somewhere in the world there is supposed to be a place from which you can walk south for 100 miles (161 km), then east for 200 miles (322 km), east, from there north for 100 miles (161 km), to arrive at the same spot from which you left. Where is that place?

Monumental

The illustrations below are the plans (seen from above and frontal view) of a monument that needs repainting. The painter bases his bid on these plans. What does the side of the monument look like?

Top view

Front view

60

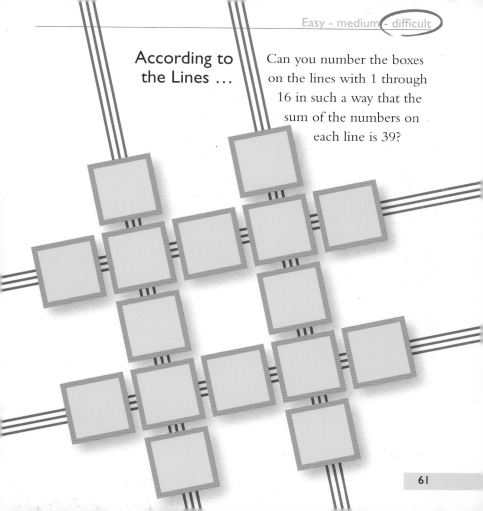

According to the Lines ...

Can you number the boxes on the lines with 1 through 16 in such a way that the sum of the numbers on each line is 39?

Secret Forces ...

Take a shot glass and bend a long
match into two halves without
breaking it. Put the match with
a coin on top of it on the glass as
illustrated on the right. Your
assignment is to drop the coin
into the glass without touching
the glass, the coin, or the match.
Can you do it?

Logic? Well, Yes …

Which letter belongs in the box with the question mark?

Chess Puzzle

Where to begin? Look for the right starting point and via knight's moves find a word of 10 letters that begins and ends with the same letter.

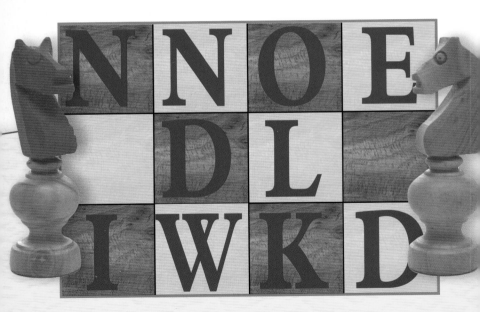

Golden Oldies ...

Below are three old vinyl records: a 33 LP, a 45, and an even
older 78. Can you estimate – accurate to the nearest
hundred – how many grooves these records have together?

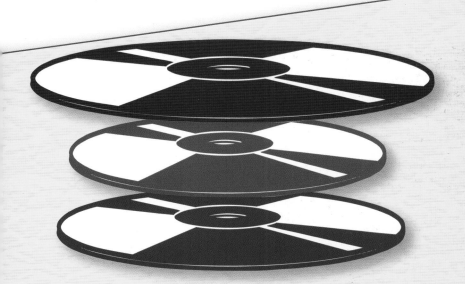

Floating in the Center ...

Fill a glass with water and take a cork. Your assignment is to keep the cork floating at the center of the water surface. Will you be able to?

Time for Prunes …

You need 10 prunes (pearl onions will do too) and 16 cocktail sticks for this puzzle. These are the materials you use to make the construction below. The assignment is: remove four cocktail sticks and one prune in such a way that you are left with five equilateral triangles.

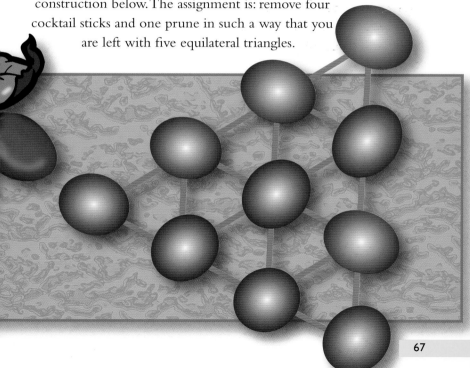

Fitting Problem

Which figure does not belong
in this puzzle set?

— C'est chez **CRÉMIEUX**, que tu as acheté un habillement aussi irréprochable?

— Oui, j'en sors, Albert devait m'attendre ici, ne l'avez-vous pas vu? — Cherchez Albert?

Searching …

Look for Albert, a friend of these people.
This is a French advertisement for the fashion brand "*Crémieux*." Paris, circa 1900.

From the collection of Jerry Slocum, USA.

The Fake Figure

Which of these five figures does not belong?

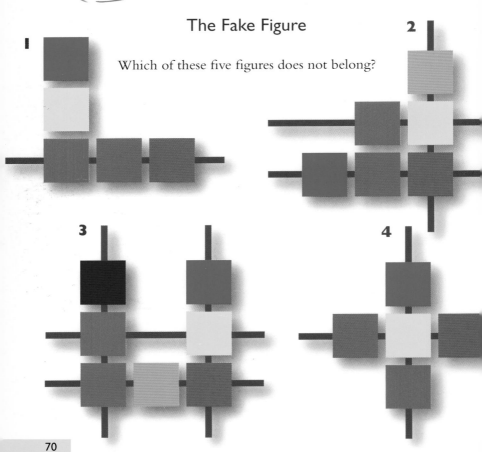

70

Next?

Finish this series of numbers.

What Does It Say?

Can you decipher this message?

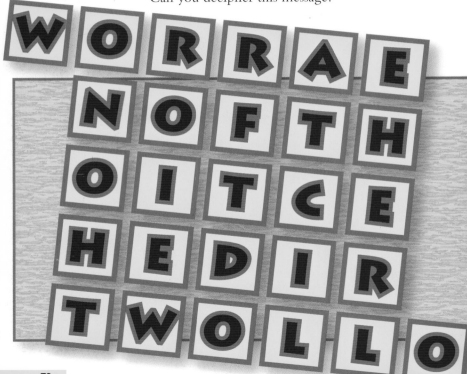

Paris

We want to go for a stroll through Paris. But where do we find a bit of nature and greenery in this city? They made a mess of it on the signpost and all the letters are mixed up!

ANDJRI UD

MGUXLEBURO

Around the Dot

Can you replace each question mark with the right number?

Jumping Out of the Rain Into …

Why do kangaroo mothers dislike rainy weather so much?

What's What?

Which number should replace the question mark?

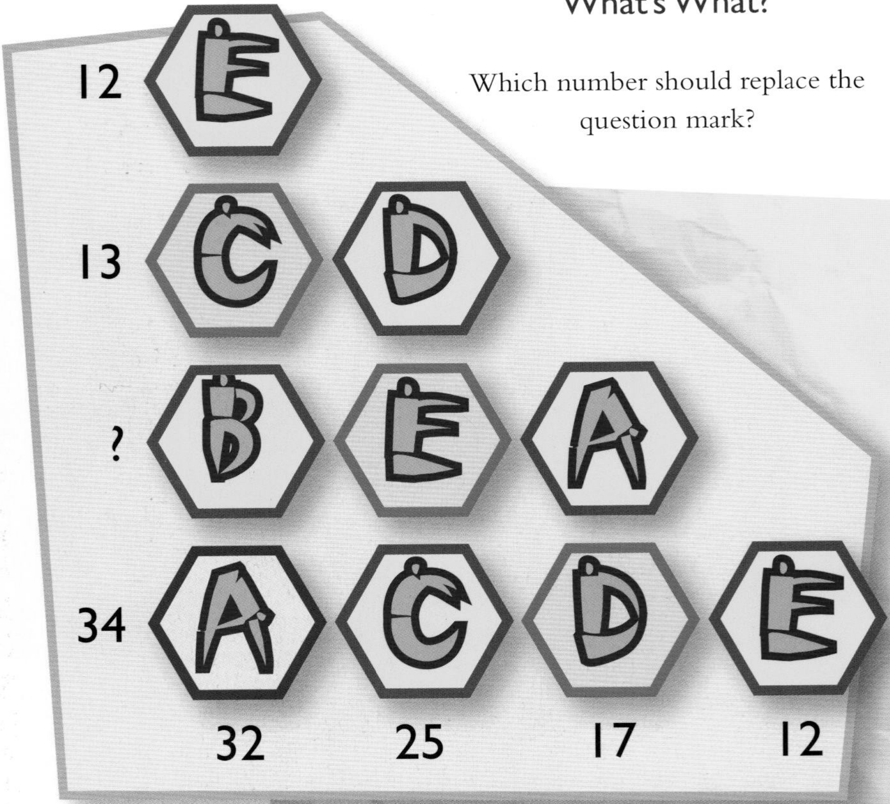

12 E

13 C D

? B E A

34 A C D E

32 25 17 12

76

Only Three …

Three rows in this grid contain exactly the same letters, but in a different order. They can be horizontal, vertical, or diagonal, but they don't have to point in the same direction. Which three rows are we talking about?

Anagrams

Well-known show biz stars.
Hint: all are men and all are deceased.
Who are they?

Ilesv Lerypse

Saft Nimodo

Knafr Rinasat

Silou Gasromrtn

Defr Rastiae

Chess Puzzle

Where to begin? Look for the right starting point and then use knight's moves to find a word of nine letters which begins and ends with the same letter.

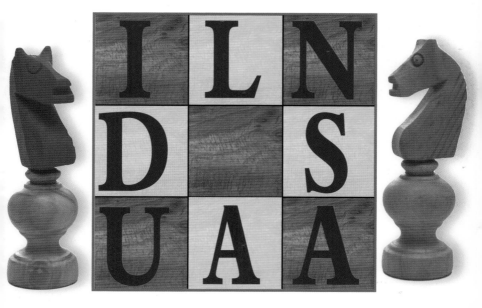

And Then …

Think logically and find the number which should replace the question mark.

French Style

Find the thief. A French advertisement from the early 1900s.

The Domino Effect

Arrange these dominos in such a way that they form the names of two well-known singers. The first name should read from left to right, the second name from right to left.

What's That For?

Sometimes you see an object that seems to
serve no purpose at all. This one is a good
example. Can you figure out what it is?

From the collection of Nanco Bordewijk, the Netherlands.

Vague Letters

Which letter should replace the question mark?

A Quick Sum ...

0000
0001
0010
0011
0100
0101
0110
0111
1000
1001
+

What is the total of these numbers?

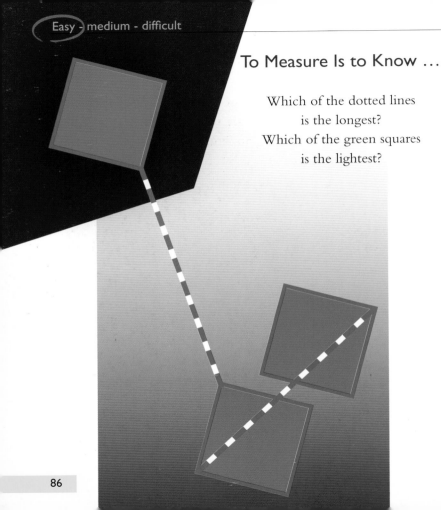

To Measure Is to Know ...

Which of the dotted lines
is the longest?
Which of the green squares
is the lightest?

Let's Bet ...

Take three glasses and position them as shown below.
In three moves, can you turn all three glasses upright?
Hint: with every move you should turn two glasses,
one in each hand.

Simple?

Which number belongs in the box with the question mark?

A Game of Cards …

What you have to do is to determine the "identity" of the playing cards below. We'll give you a few hints.

1. There is at least one 3 to the right of a 2.
2. There is at least one spade to the right of another spade.
3. There is at least one 3 to the left of a 3
4. There is at least one spade directly to the left of a diamond.

So which card is where?

World Tour

Jack Jones made a world tour in his new car, a trip of 25,000 miles (40,000 km). His one spare tire he had rotated over the four wheels so that each tire had "a rest." Afterward Jack discovered that all five tires were equally worn. Can you calculate how much distance each tire covered on the road?

Tricky ...

Two rows of numbers.
Can you exchange two
numbers in such a way that
the rows add up to the same
total? Right now the totals
are 19 and 20.

1
2
7
9

3
4
5
8

Brainteaser ...

Which number should replace the question mark?

16 ? 24

14 8 6

16 12 8

Hidden Secrets ...

This American postcard from 1890 hides six figures: a cage, a mouse, an eel, an Indian, a trowel, and a basket. The initial letters of these words represented the slogan of the company.

Clarck's **M**ile **E**nd **is** **t**he **b**est.

Cage, **M**ouse, **E**el, **I**ndian, **T**rowell, **B**asket.

From the collection of Jerry Slocum, USA.

The Chopstick Problem ...

Recently after dinner at a Chinese restaurant seven beans were left on my plate. As I had liked the dish very much, the owner promised me another one if, with three chopsticks, I was able to divide the plate in seven sections holding one bean each. Do you feel like Chinese food?

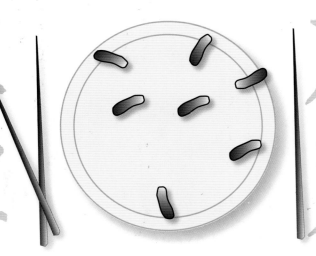

Chinese Game of Cards

Pick three of these cards but in such a way that you have a total of three hearts, three diamonds, three spades, and three clubs.

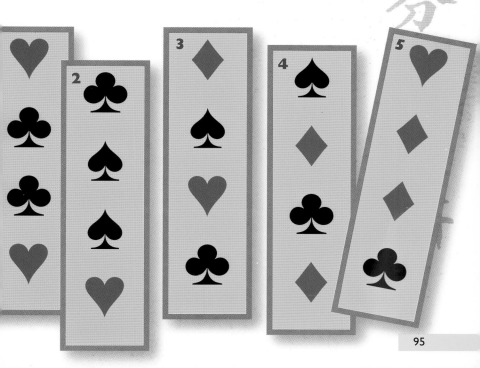

Chess Puzzle

Where to begin? Look for the right starting point, and via knight's moves find a word of nine letters. The first and last letter of this word should be the same.

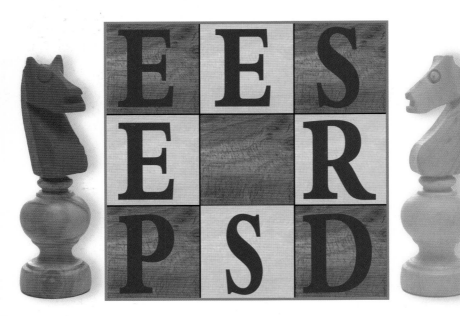

Crosswise

There are a couple of ways in which you can make a square out of these four figures.

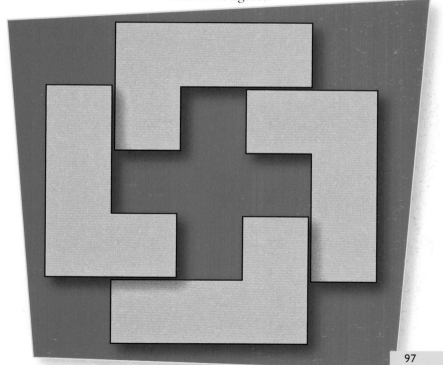

Logic!

Which numbers should replace the question marks?

How Pretty She Is!

This lady has gone through no less that seven husbands.
Can you find them?

From the collection of Jerry Slocum, United States

Musical Anagrams

Seven famous composers, albeit a little confused. But pay attention: all the names have one letter too many. And with those seven extra letters you can "compose" the name of yet another composer.

VANWERG

HABCI

PONHIAC

NOHVEDE-BET

YSVUDSEB

HALLREM

HIRSBAM

Impressive Horse Race

Two friends, each owner of a race horse, made an unusual bet: not the first horse at the finish would win the race, but the horse finishing second.

The two begin the race and go as fast as they can until about the last 100 yards (about 91½ m). Then they start riding slower and slower, until they conclude this bet does not work. They ask the advice of a farmer they meet on the road. The farmer gives them good advice, whereupon the two men dash back to their horses and ride them as hard as they can. What was the farmer's tip?

Pointy Problem

Can you lay down these nails in such a way
that all the nails touch each other?

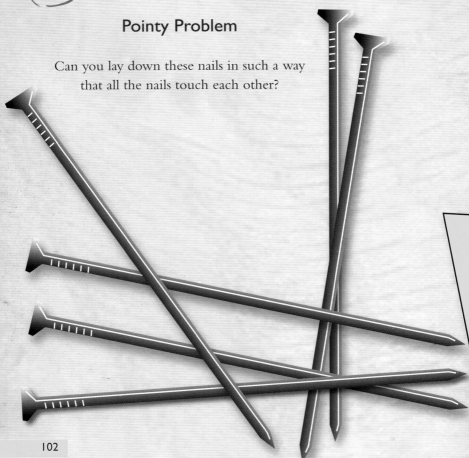

The Local Cop

The squares below represent blocks of houses in a city neighborhood. Lieutenant Trigger-Happy has to patrol this neighborhood every evening. For this purpose he devised a route enabling him to check all the windows on the different sides of the houses without once crossing the route. Can you figure out what his route is?

Cheers!

Hmm, they're looking good, those beers! The inside measurements of the large glass are twice those of the small glass. How many times do you have to pour the contents of the small glass into the large glass to completely fill the large glass?

What's That For?

Sometimes you see an object that seems to serve
no purpose at all.
This one is a good example.
Can you figure out what it is?

From the collection of Nanco Bordewijk, the Netherlands.

Lewis Carroll's Paradox

It was Lewis Carroll, the famous author of Alice in Wonderland, who thought up this impossible puzzle. The surface of this cut-up square encompasses 64 small squares. But if you make a rectangle out of the pieces (see next page), the surface becomes 65 small squares. How is this possible?

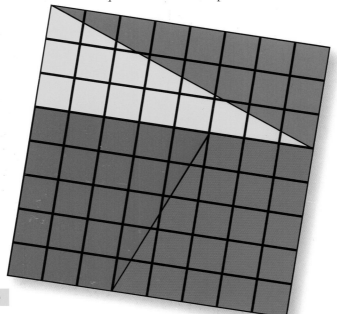

Capering Around

A neat row of 15 matches, right? But we want you to disturb this neat row, for your assignment is to regroup the matches into five little heaps of three matches. You do this by having a match jump three other matches each time.

1
2
3
4
5
6
7
8
9
10
11
12
13
14
15

124

Calculating

Do you have a calculator? Then do the following. Enter the number that's twice your age. Add five to that. Multiply by 50. Add to this the sum of the coins (less than one dollar) in your wallet or pocket. Deduct the number of days in the year (365) from the total, add 115 to the result, and then divide the total by 100. The result gives four digits (if you're older than ten). The two digits before the decimal point represent your age. The two after represent the sum of the coins in your pocket.

Age Difference

Two weeks ago my sister was twice as old as I was at that moment. In eight years, the sum of our ages will be 50. How old am I now?

Nosing Around …

How many noses do you count?
A nose is only a nose if it has a
face attached to it.

A Logical Sequence

Which letter replaces the question mark?

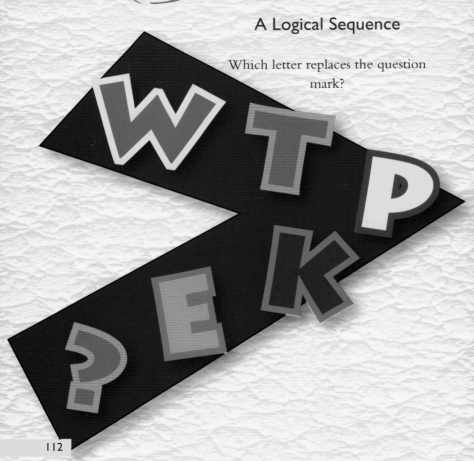

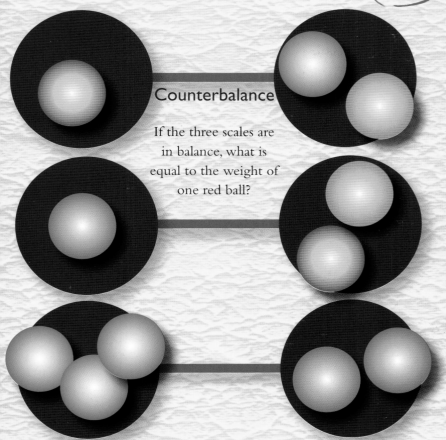

Counterbalance

If the three scales are in balance, what is equal to the weight of one red ball?

A Puzzle Chain ...

Brace yourself! The following eight pages of this book form a chain of puzzles. What it is? It's very simple ... you need the solution of the first puzzle to be able to solve the puzzle on the next page. In other words, you need the solution of the puzzle on this page to solve the one on page 115, and so on. But what if your solution is wrong? Well ...

Puzzle 1

If six boys need six exercise books in six weeks and four girls need four exercise books in four weeks, how many exercise books does a class of 12 boys and 12 girls need in 12 weeks?

Puzzle 2

Which number belongs in the box with the question mark?

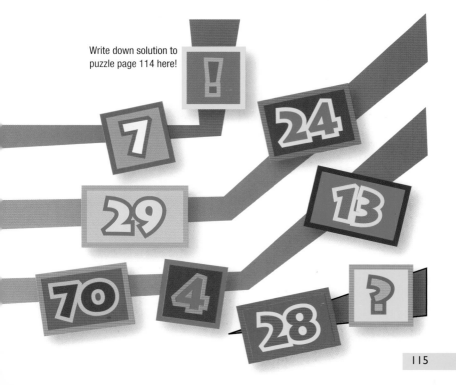

Write down solution to puzzle page 114 here!

!

7

24

29

13

70

4

28

?

Puzzle 3

Which number should replace the question mark?

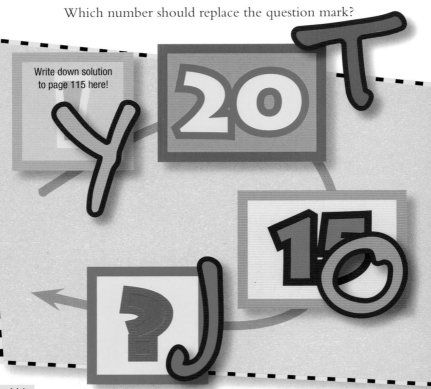

Write down solution to page 115 here!

Puzzle 4

Shopping…
If I start with $?
and spend everything
except $3, how much do
I have left?

Write down solution to page 116 here!

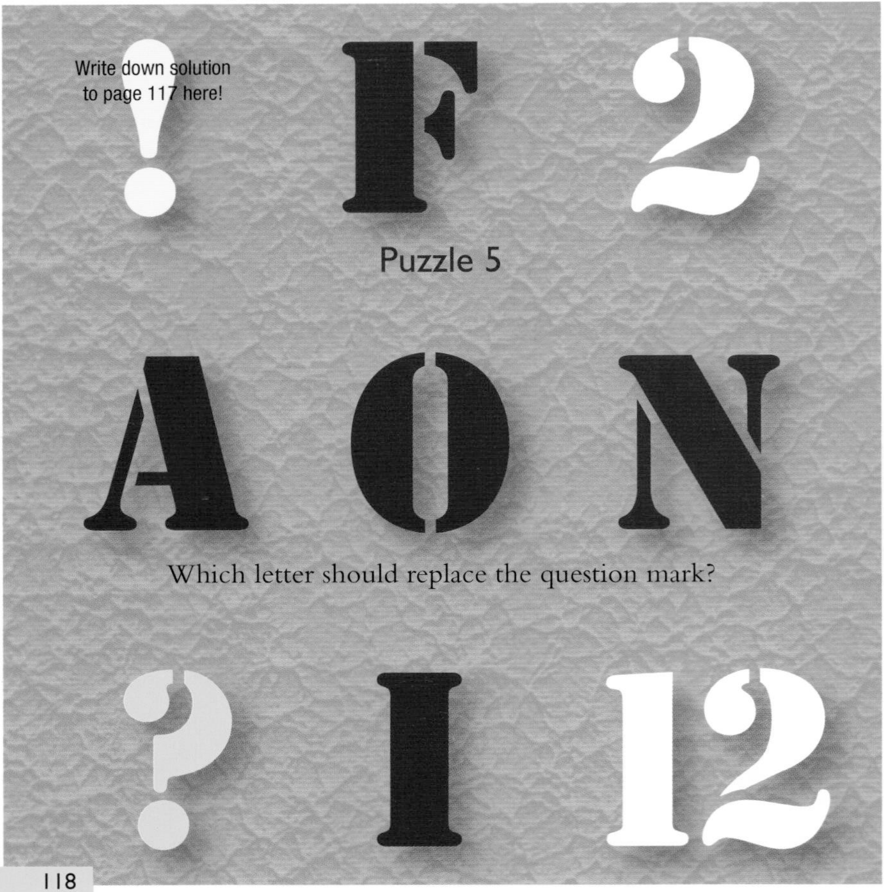

! **F** **2**

Write down solution to page 117 here!

Puzzle 5

A **O** **N**

Which letter should replace the question mark?

? **I** **12**

Puzzle 6

A break of a few days … We'd like to take one, but someone has mixed up the letters of the name of our destination. Can you figure out which state we're going to?

Write down solution to page 118 here!

Puzzle 7

Write down the fourth letter of solution to page 119 here!

Which letter does not belong here?

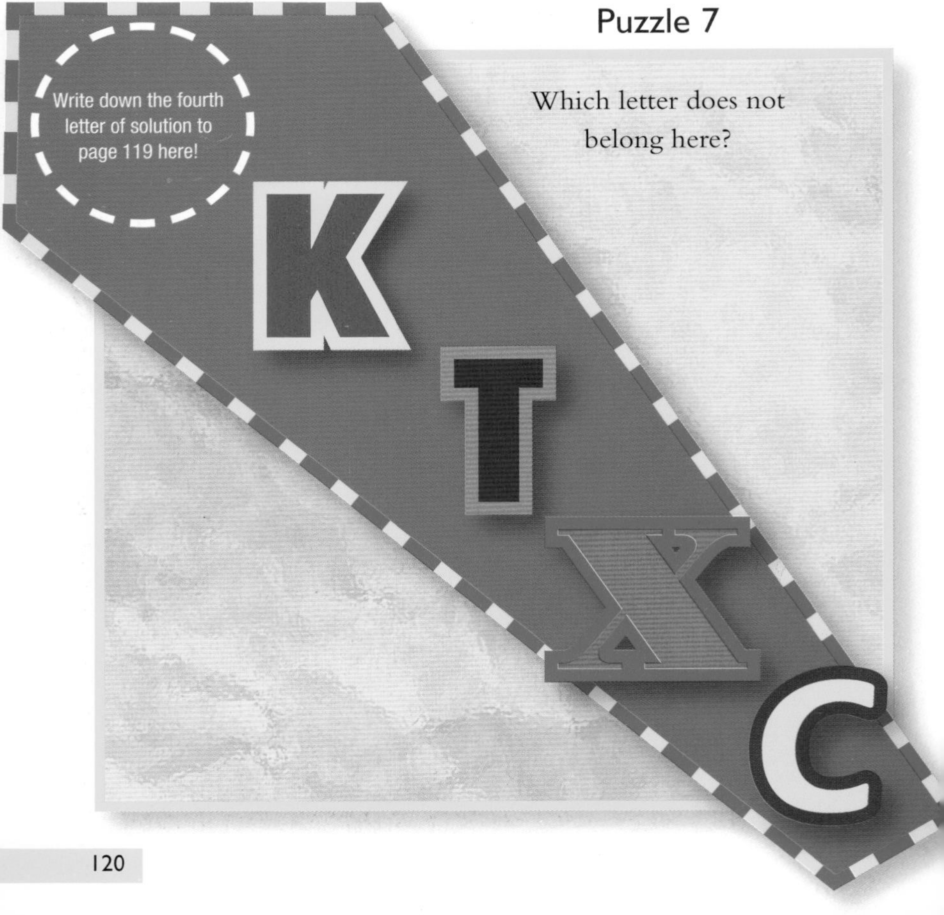

K

T

X

C

Puzzle 8

The last one…
Imitate the letter with the help of two match-es. Then take another two matches and do the same. With these two shapes you can make a square.

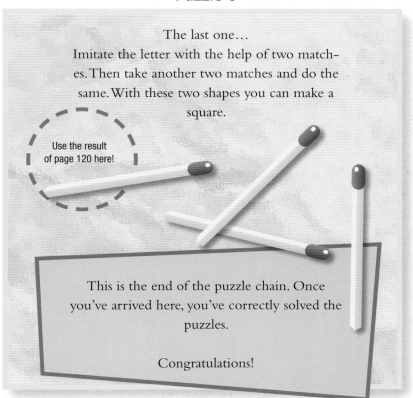

Use the result of page 120 here!

This is the end of the puzzle chain. Once you've arrived here, you've correctly solved the puzzles.

Congratulations!

The Exception

Which figure does not belong in the group below?

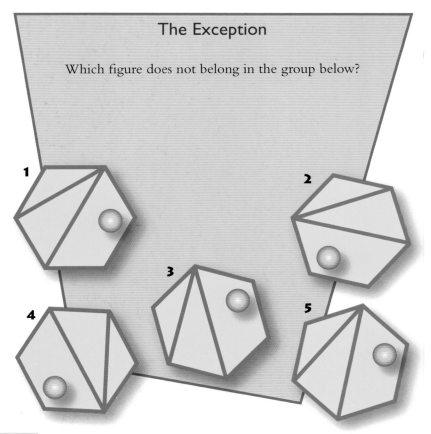

The Sentence

The lord of the castle sentenced one of his servants to death for stealing jewelry. But because he felt some compassion for the servant, he allowed him to determine the manner of execution. What kind of death did the servant choose?

From 8 to 10

With the letters below, form a word of ten letters, beginning and ending with the same letter. Also, two letters are used twice.

MOSCHELES

Allegro

Multi-Musical ...

What's so special about this sheet of music?

Triangles!

How many triangles do you count here?

Central Problem

Which letter should replace the question mark?

What's That For?

Sometimes you see an object that seems to serve
no purpose at all. This one is a good example.
Can you figure out what it is?

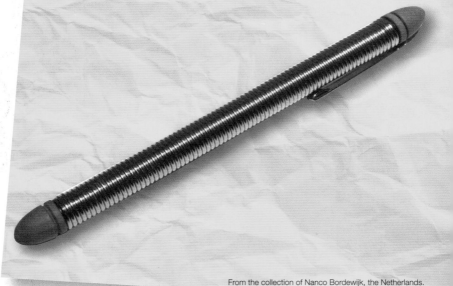

From the collection of Nanco Bordewijk, the Netherlands.

What's Next?

Compare the changes in the sequence of figures below.
Do you know what figure 6 should look like?

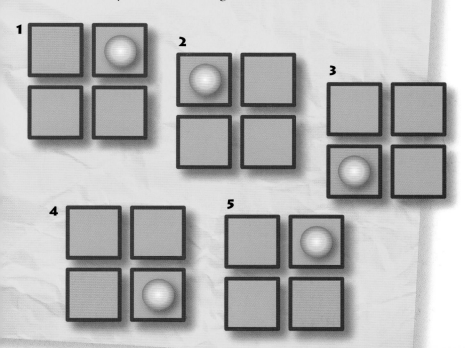

LA Daytrip

We'd like to do a tour of Los Angeles. But where should we go for a special town bordering this big city? They've made a mess of the name on the signpost – there's an I missing and no less than two times the O!

Chess Puzzle

Where to begin? Look for the right starting point and via knight's moves find a word of nine letters with the same first and last letter.

This is a well-known city in England.

Logic!

Which number should replace the question mark?

Friday the Thirteenth …

Bad luck day, a day for accidents….
In an average period of a number of years,
how many times is Friday a 13th of the
month?

I See, I See, What You See Too …

Which arrow is lighter?

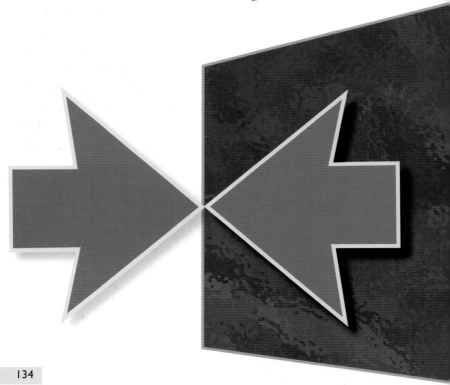

Question from the Cross ...

Illustrated here is a cross made up of coins. It has nine coins in the vertical row, nine coins from the bottom to the outside coin of the left arm, and nine coins from the bottom to the outside coin of the right arm. By removing two coins and moving two coins, can you make a cross with exactly the same properties?

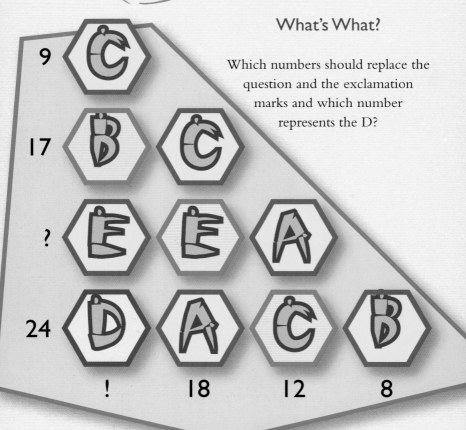

What's What?

Which numbers should replace the question and the exclamation marks and which number represents the D?

9

17

?

24

!   18   12   8

Math Genius ...

Add the number 2 to 191 and arrive at an answer that's less than 20.

Halfhearted 1

Find the horse's back half.

Halfhearted 2

Find the witch's crow.

Picture puzzles
from France, late
nineteenth century.

From the collection of Jerry Slocum, USA.

A Pattern

Place the numbers 1 through 8 in the boxes in such a way that the
numbers differing by one (like 2 and 3) are not connected
by a line.

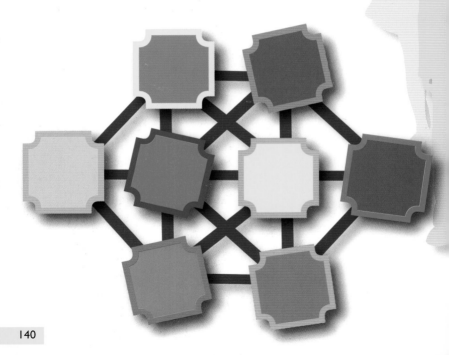

Family Puzzle

A man and a woman have four married daughters, who each have four children. All the members of these three generations are still alive. How many people were present when all the three generations came to the family reunion?

A Birthday

Today it's Miriam's birthday. The day after tomorrow it's the birthday of Monique, her twin sister. How is this possible?

Next?

Logically speaking, what should figure 4 look like?

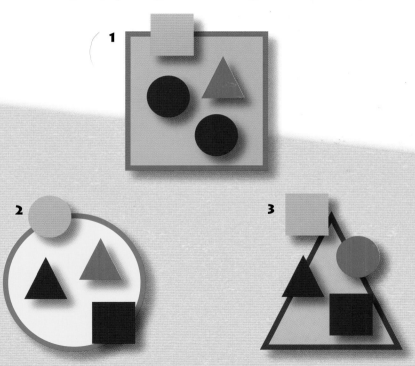

Strange Sum …

Which number should replace the question mark?

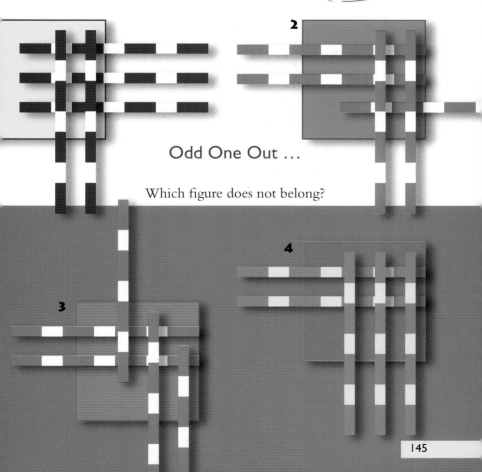

Odd One Out …

Which figure does not belong?

2

3

4

What's That For?

Sometimes you see an object that seems to serve no
purpose at all. This one is a good example.
Can you figure out what it is?

bcfghjklmopqrvwxyz

A Different Kind of Anagram …

Above are the letters you don't need, but the rest of the alphabet you do need to form a name of 12 letters! Find out which letters they are and put them in the right order. Two letters are used twice and one other letter is used three times.

Hint: hamburgers and milkshakes.

147

V, W, and X

There are three letters in this diagram. Add a total of seven of these letters in such a way that each horizontal and each vertical row has one of each of the three.

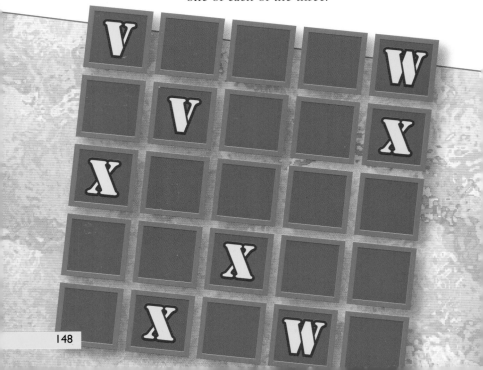

Leading Anagrams

Five famous leaders, albeit a little mixed up — that is
to say, the letters of their names are. Can you
reorder them so we know who these leaders are?

Laresch ed Lageul

Siluju Raacse

Mbarhaa Ninlloc

Dicarhr Xonin

Arsofniç Terndatim

149

Lost Letters

Which letters belong in the boxes with question marks?

Far Away …

Can you decipher the name of the country we're referring to?

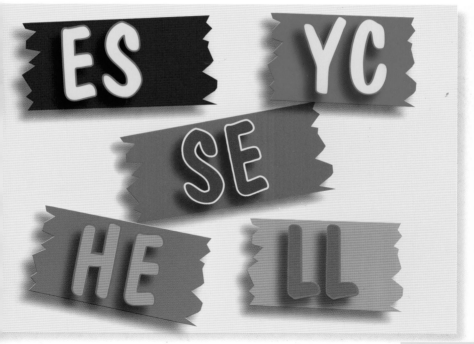

Broken Letters

Copy and cut out the pieces and make them into a square.
The pieces can also be turned around.

Where to Begin?

Which numbers belong in the boxes with question marks?

Singing in the Rain …

John was taken by surprise by a rain shower. He was without an umbrella, hat, or anything else to cover his head and he could not find a place to shelter.

He stood there for 15 minutes, in the pouring rain. When he finally was able to hail a taxi, his hair had not gotten wet.

How's that possible?

Cannon Fodder

With the cannonballs on the next page, how many more do you need to make an exact pyramid?

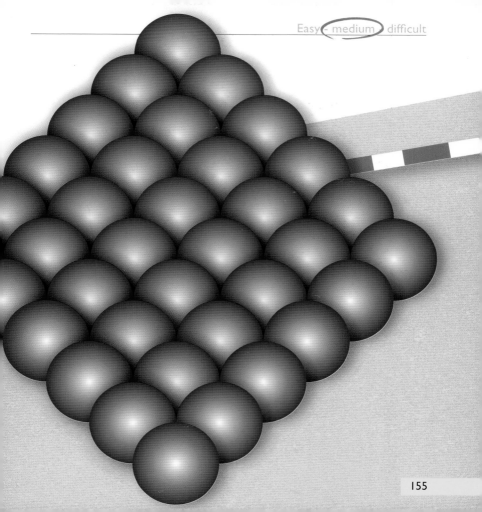

Chess Puzzle

Where to begin? Look for the right starting point and via knight's moves find a word of 10 letters that begins and ends with the same letter.

Taxi!

You should be able to read this short story within 30 seconds. And only 30 seconds are needed to test your observational powers.

A lady gets into a taxi. The taxi leaves. The lady starts to talk. The driver doesn't like passengers who talk to him. He thinks quickly, and mimes the fact that he is deaf. He points at his mouth, and shakes his head. He points at his ears and again shakes his head. The lady stops talking. Arriving at her destination, she realizes she's been made a fool of. How did she find out? The meter showed the price and the driver never said a word.

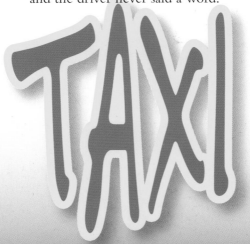

One Cub Too Many …

How many times does a tigress walk back and forth, beginning at the new den, to take five cubs to that new den, if she transports one cub at a time?

Self-Evident?

Which number should replace
the question mark?

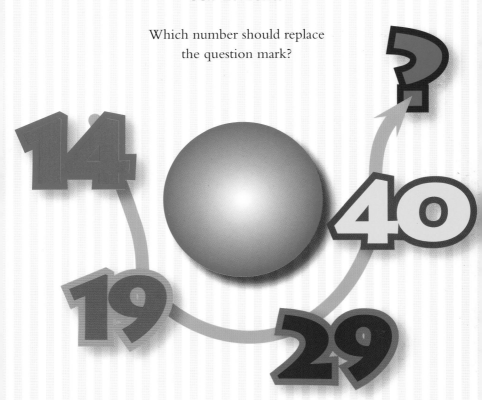

What's That For?

Sometimes you see an object that seems to serve
no purpose at all.
This one is a good example. Can you figure out
what it is?

From the collection of Nanco Bordewijk, the Netherlands.

160

Famous Movie Stars

These five famous and trigger-happy movie stars are a little mixed up. That is to say, the letters of their names are. Can you order them in such a way that we know who we mean?

Ticnl Ostawoed

Lasechr Sornnob

Honj Ynewa

Racy Trang

Ubrec Sliwil

Domino Sums ...

With a double three set you can make the pyramid below in such a
way that the total of the dots on the stones in the rows and columns
becomes what is indicated by the numbers.

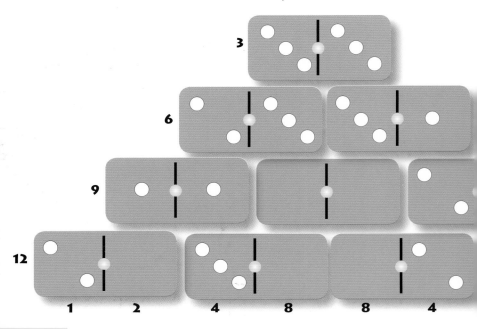

$$.... \div .. = ...$$

.0

.3

3.

A Bit of Calculating...

A four-digit number is divided by a two-digit number. The result is a four-digit number.
Only three numbers are used.
Do you know which ones?

..

.0

1

Domino Games

Order these domino pictures in such a way that the names of two well-known aircraft are created. The top one read from left to right and the one below it from right to left.

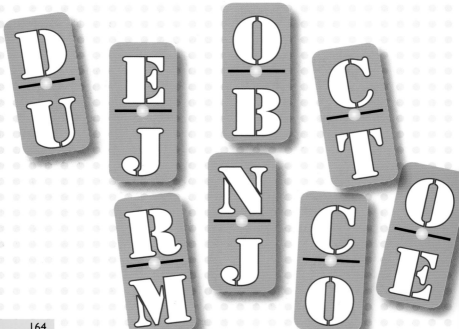

Divide and Rule …

Use four straight lines to
divide the page into nine
fields inside which
the total of the
numbers is 20 …

To See Is to Eat?

Move your nose toward the arrow and you'll easily work up an appetite.

From the collection of Jerry Slocum, United States.

Making the Connection …

Connect the same letters by lines. Then place the numbers 1 through 9 in the squares, but in such a way that the total of the numbers per line is 13.

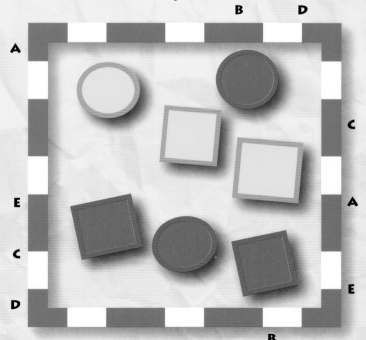

A Drinking Problem ...

Put six glasses in a row. Numbers 3, 4, and 5 are full. Now reorder
the glasses in such a way that the first empty glass is followed by a
full one, and then in turn empty and full glasses. The only problem
is, you may only touch and move one glass.

Impolite ...

A man would like to know the age of the charming woman he's having a drink with, but he's too much of a gentleman to ask her directly. Yet there is way to find out without hurting the feelings of the lady in question. All she needs to disclose is her height. How do you discover her age?

4

5

6

Fair and Square ...

Two fathers and two sons win the amount of $630,000 in the state lottery. After having divided the money into equal parts, each of them goes home with $210,000. How's this possible?

Big, Bigger, Biggest ...

The two clowns on the next page are clearly different in size. Or are they?

From the collection of Jerry Slocum, USA.

In the Days of Yore

Once these ladies were big movie stars, but that's a long time ago. Who remembers their names?

Trage Rogba

Noesmi Gostiern

Eurday Phneurb

Neemlar Ehricidt

Ema Twes

Soup Chicken?

This chicken's owner feels like having chicken soup, so a tragic end is in store for the poor bird. But where is the owner?

From the collection of Jerry Slocum, USA.

Next?

Which number should replace
the question mark?

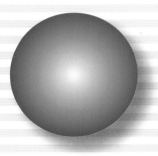

Turning This Way and That

Does the top left blue square fit between the red squares on the right and below?

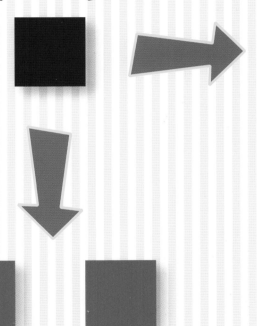

Burning Problem

Move three matches and make eight triangles.

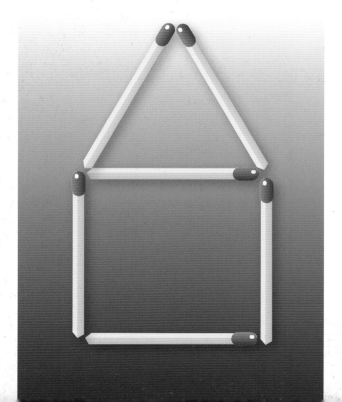

Fitting Together Exactly

Which four pieces can you fit together so they make a square?

What Is Missing?

Which number belongs on the spot where the question mark is now?

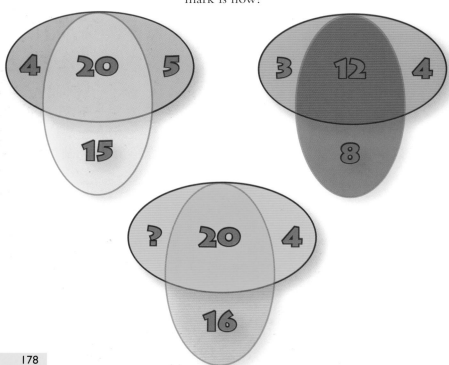

Pears and Lemons, Anyone?

Six pears and nine lemons cost $1.17.
Five pears and eleven lemons cost $1.29.
How much does one lemon cost? And how much one pear?

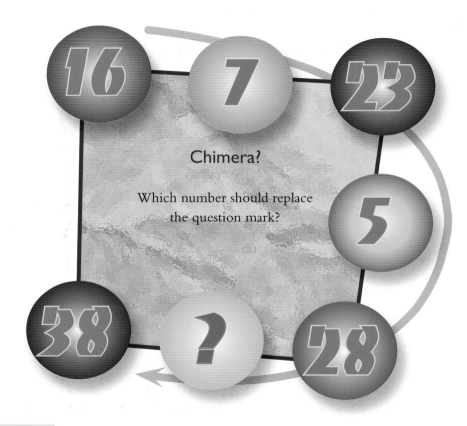

Chimera?

Which number should replace
the question mark?

Brainy

Which number belongs on the spot with the question mark?

A Good Eye

These three pieces together can form an object. Just by looking at them, can you determine what this object looks like?

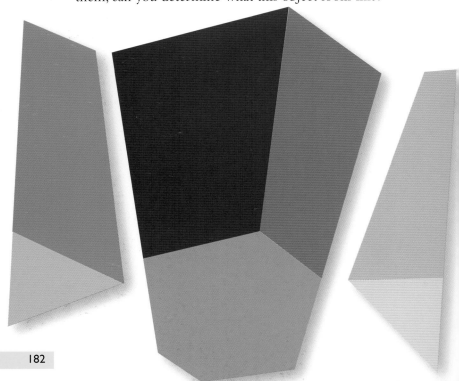

Wedding Party

One woman married 15
different people in
one day.
How is this possible?

Coin Puzzle

You need nine coins of the same size for this puzzle. Lay them down into a triangle as shown below left. Then, by only moving one coin at a time, make the figure below right.
And to make it a bit more difficult for you: each coin you have moved must always touch two others.

Geometry

Divide this figure into eight sections with the same size and shape.

Each of these

sections
should have
only one
red and
one blue
ball.

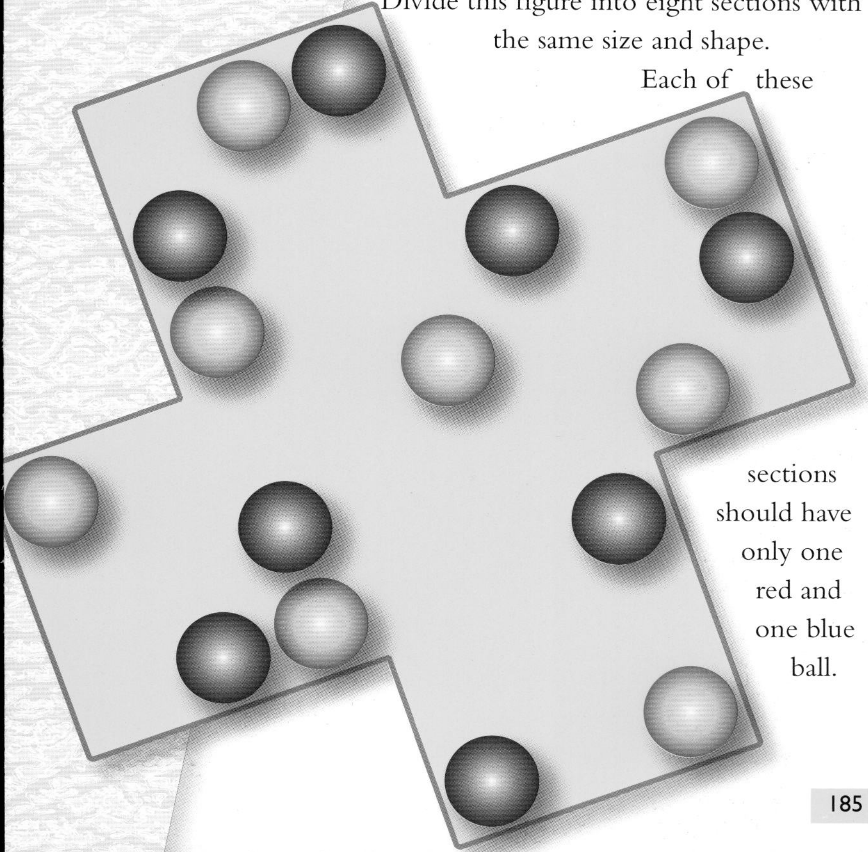

Baseball

You have to answer the question immediately.

A player buys a new baseball bat and ball for $125. The bat costs $25 more than the ball. What does each of them cost?

Broken Letters

Copy and cut out the pieces and make a square of them.

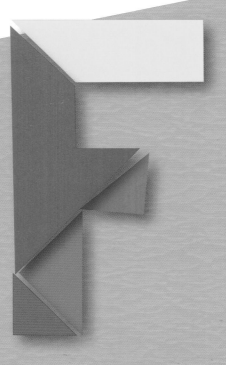

What's That For?

Sometimes you see an object that seems to serve no purpose at all. This one is a good example. Can you figure out what it is?

From the collection of Nanco Bordewijk, the Netherlands.

Hidden Letters

Which letters belong in the squares with question marks?

SOLUTIONS

No Trespassing

Penal Code Art. 007

P. 8 Ink Blots

Mail Box

Envelope

P. 9 Illusion

Yes, it's the same color over the whole width. Block out the space around it with a piece of paper to make sure.

P. 10 A Sharp-Witted Square

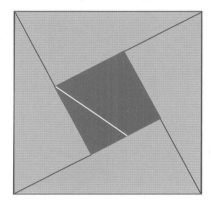

P. 11 "Lay-Down" Puzzle

16 rows with an even number of coins.

P. 12 Only Three ...

P. 13 New York
Central Park.

P. 14 Dogs ...
More than the dog knows!

P. 15 What's What?
70. The numbers, represented by the letters, are multiplied.

P. 16 Sign Language
Good morning.

P. 17 Secret Language?
It's raining cats and dogs!
Follow the direction of the arrow.

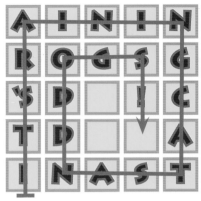

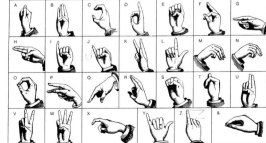
American Sign Language manual alphabet

P. 18 Logic!

2. The sum of the numbers along the lines is 13.

P. 19 Find the Animal

P. 20 Hopscotch

The relationship between the numbers is as indicated below.

2+8=10, 10×2=20
7+5=12, 12×7=84
4+3=7, 7×4=28

P. 21 Famous Saying?

The legibility of a letter depends on the upper half of it.

two
beer
or
not
two
beer
William
Shakebeer

P. 22 Politicians Sleep the Sleep of the Dead …

Theodore Roosevelt
Gerald Ford
Winston Churchill
Golda Meir
Richard Nixon

P. 23 Marbles

17. The numbers of the other marbles add up to 9.

P. 24 Cut Up!

The first small icon is the same as the big one before, the second is always the same, the third is the icon itself, and the fourth is the next big icon.

P. 25 Well-Known Names

Bernard
Rambo
Elvis

The codes refer to the position of the letters in the square.
The columns are U through Z, the rows 1 through 5.
Example: U1 is A, V4 is Q, and so on.

P. 26 Blowing Test

Place the book on a strong paper or plastic bag and blow air into the bag. An illustration from a U.S. booklet on physics experiments, circa 1910.

P. 27 Magical Matches

Put a drop of water on where the matches were broken and they will "make" a star themselves.

P. 28 Question Mark

The L. The letters represent their position in the alphabet. The letter in the third column minus the one in the second is the letter in the first.

P. 29 Chess Puzzle

Nonfiction

P. 30 Just Out for a Sec …

P. 31 Pointed Affair

You can make 20 rectangles and squares. The two everyone forgets are shown here.

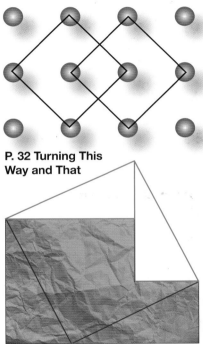

P. 32 Turning This Way and That

P. 33 Backward Sports?

Backstroke in swimming
Tug of War
Rowing

P. 34 The Connection ...

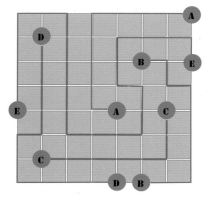

P. 35 King ...?

DAVID. D is the Roman numeral for
500. V represents the 5. The first of the
letters is the A and the first of the numbers is the 1 (in this case the Roman 1).

P. 36 Closed Squares

A=2
B=11
C=8
D=1
E=14
F=4
H=13
I=5
J=9

P. 37 Light in the Darkness ...

They're both equally light. See for
yourself: cover the page with a piece of
paper with two holes in it where the
circles are.

P. 38 The Odd One Out ...

4. The other figures each have a ball
touching both of their planes.

P. 39 Just 15 …

P. 40 Gravity …

Cut the paper into a coin shape but one size smaller than the coin. Put the piece of paper on the coin. See to it the coin is exactly horizontal and drop both at the same time.

Thanks to the suction power of the coin the piece of paper will stick to it.

P. 41 Next …

J. The letters represent their position in the alphabet. Thus, based on this position, certain relationships between the letters are created.

N+2=P
P-5=K
K+2=M
M-5=H
H+2=J

The recurring elements are +2 and -5.

P. 42 Love Is Blind

Look through your eyelashes and you'll see why.

P. 43 Logistic Anagrams

**AMSTERDAM
NEW YORK
LOS ANGELES
BARCELONA
MADRID
ROME**

P. 44 Type Case …

The letters are in alphabetical order in the direction of the arrow, except that two letters are skipped each time.

P. 45 Torture

4444÷40=111.1

P. 46 Water Running Uphill

The flame uses up the oxygen in the glass, reducing the pressure and making the water rise.

From a booklet published in 1910 in the United States.

P. 47 Logic!

2. It concerns the difference between the numbers along the lines and in the direction of the arrows.

So 16-4-3=9, 9-3-4=2, 16-4-10=2, and so on.

P. 48 That Poor Woman!

P. 49 Brainteaser

1. The numbers in the upper row minus the numbers of the lower row all have nine as a result per column. The same applies from right to left in all the rows.

P. 50 What's That For?

To cut off egg tops.

P. 51 Capital

Paris (position in the alphabet but four letters farther and written backward).

P. 52 Logical Numbering

1. From 3 on, the two following numbers add up to the previous number by adding or subtracting. 3=4-1, 4=1+3, 1=4-3, 3=4-1, 4=3+1, 1=3-2, 2=3-1.

P. 53 The Joke(r) Is on You ...

Cut open a playing card on the lines and carefully pull it open so you can crawl through it.

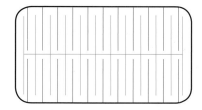

P. 54 15, 16, and 17 ...

15 and 16 go into the blue shape, 17 into the green one. The yellow shape has only numbers formed by round lines, the green shape numbers are formed by straight lines, and the blue shape numbers have round and straight lines.

P. 55 Patching up a Quarrel ...

Lay down the handkerchief over the threshold of an open door. Ask your opponent to stand on the edge of the handkerchief, on the other side of the door. Then close the door, lock it, and stand on the handkerchief on your side of the door. Now use your mental powers to convince your opponent of the fact that you are right.

P. 56 Star Puzzle
G. Each letter opposite another is worth twice what the latter is worth, looked at from their position in the alphabet.
A=1, B opposite it = 2.
J=10, T opposite it = 20.

P. 57 Turning This Way and That
Number 4.

P. 58 Famous Race Tracks
132. The sum of the position of the letters in the alphabet.

He is riding toward you if that's the way you want it, but away from you is also possible. It's a question of how you look at it.

P. 59 Quite a Walk …
The only place is the North Pole, beginning from the North Pole.

P. 60 Monumental

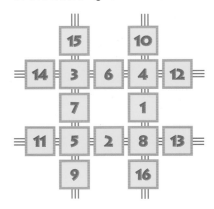

Side view

P. 61 According to the Lines …

P. 62 Secret Forces …

Let one or two drops of water fall on the bend in the match. After a few moments the match will straighten and the coin will drop in the glass.

P. 63 Logic? Well, Yes …

S. There is a logical sequence, beginning with A, based on the position on the alphabet, in the direction of the arrow. +2, -4, and so on. A comes after the Z.

P. 64 Chess Puzzle

Downlinked.

P. 65 Golden Oldies …

3. Each disc has only one groove, which spirals to the center.

P. 66 Floating in the Center …

Fill the glass until the water is just above its rim. Carefully deposit the cork in the water – it will float directly to the "highest point," i.e., the middle.

P. 67 Time for Prunes …

P. 68 Fitting Problem

No. 2.

P. 69 Searching …

— C'est chez CRÉMIEUX, que tu as acheté un habillement aussi irréprochable ?
— Oui, j'en sors; Albert devait m'attendre ici, ne l'avez-vous pas vu ? — Cherchez Albert ?

P. 70 The Fake Figure

No. 3. It's the only figure with three times three squares in a row. The red lines correspond with the number of the sequence.

P. 71 Next?

68. The number that's inside a circle is multiplied by 2. Five is added to the number inside a square . The next one is 63 plus 5.

P. 72 What Does It Say?

Followthedirectionofthearrow. Exactly!

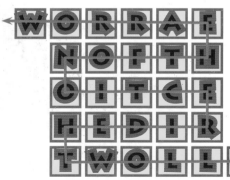

P. 73 Paris

Jardin du Luxembourg.

P. 74 Around the Dot

The numbers at the end of a line are added up, plus 2. The solution can be found in the middle box of each line. 4+1(+2)=7.

P. 75 Jumping Out of the Rain …

Because then her young ones then have to play inside.

P. 76 What's What?
27. The numbers, represented by the symbols, are added up.

P. 77 Only Three …

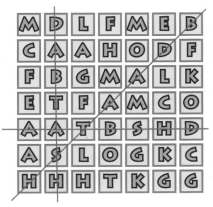

P. 78 Anagrams
Elvis Presley
Fats Domino
Frank Sinatra
Louis Armstrong
Fred Astaire

P. 79 Chess Puzzle
Andalusia.

P. 80 And Then …
7. The number in the box is multiplied by the number of balls above the box after which the number of balls below the box is subtracted.

P. 81 French Style

P. 82 The Domino Effect

P. 83 What's That For?

To cut out grapefruit segments.

P. 84 Vague Letters

C. The letters represent their position in the alphabet (A=1, B=2, etc.). The top row and the middle row (added up, subtracted, and multiplied, respectively) is the bottom row. Thus, the result is always 9.

P. 85 A Quick Sum ...

45. The numbers represent the binary umbers 0 through 9.

P. 86 To Measure Is to Know ...

The two lines are the same length. The squares are the same color green.

P. 87 Let's Bet ...

A. Turn glasses 1 and 2 upside down.
B. Turn glasses 1 and 3 upside down.
C. Turn glasses 1 and 2 upside down.

P. 88 Simple?

14. It's a magical square, which means that all the columns, rows, and diagonals add up to the same total, in this case 34.

P. 89 A Game of Cards ...

A. Two of spades.
B. Three of spades.
C. Three of diamonds.

P. 90 World Tour

Since each tire has been used 4/5 of the trip, each tire has covered 80% of 25,000 miles (40,000 km) or 20,000 miles (32,000 km).

P. 91 Tricky ...

Put the 9 in the column of the 8 and vice versa. Then turn the 9 around so it becomes a 6. We told you it was "tricky" ...

P. 92 Brainteaser

20 or 4. The difference between the numbers at the far ends of the diagonals, and the difference between the numbers at the far ends of the middle column and middle row, is 8.

P. 93 Hidden Secrets ...

HIDDEN OBJECTS.
FIND THE OBJECTS CONCEALED IN THE PICTURE.
CAGE, MOUSE, EEL, INDIAN, TROWEL, BASKET.

98

P. 94 The Chopstick Problem

P. 95 Chinese Game of Cards

Numbers. 2, 3 and 5.

P. 96 Chess Puzzle

Depressed.

P. 97 Crosswise

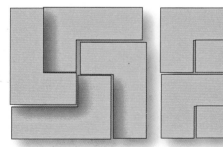

P. 98 Logic!

12 and 15. The numbers in the boxes connected by a blue line add up to 15.

P. 99 How Pretty She Is!

P. 100 Musical Anagrams

Wagner
Bach
Chopin
Beethoven
Debussy
Mahler
Brahms
Extra name: Vivaldi.

P. 101 Impressive Horse Race

The bet was that the second "horse"
would win. The farmer advised them to
ride each other's horse to the finish.

P. 102 Pointy Problem ...

P. 103 The Local Cop

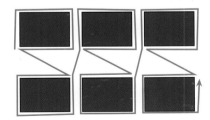

P. 104 Cheers!

Eight times. If all the inside measurements of a glass are doubled, the volume is 8 times more.

For example: if you double the 1×1×1 inches (or 1×1×1 cm) to 2×2×2 inches (or 2×2×2 cm) the volume becomes 8 inches^3 (or 8 cm^3).

P. 105 What's That For?

You clean the glasses of your spectacles with it.

P. 106-107 Lewis Carroll's Paradox

When you put the pieces on the 5×13 plane, in reality a crack is created on the diagonal – due to the deviation of the corner of the diagonal – which is equal to the surface of one square.

P. 108 Capering Around

2 on 6

1 on 6

8 on 12

7 on 12

9 on 5

10 on 5

4 between 5 and 6

3 between 5 and 6

11 between 5 and 6

13 on 11

14 on 11

15 on 11

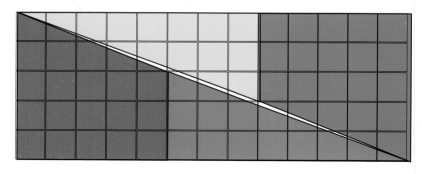

P. 109 Calculating

It's always fun to bet with someone you know about the amount of cash in one's pocket.

P. 110 Age Difference

X is the age of the youngest, five years ago. The sister was 2X years old at the time. Today they are X + 5 and 2X + 5, respectively. In eight years they will be X + 13 and 2X + 13. The total is 3X + 26 years at that moment.

3X + 26 = 50, 3X=24, X=8. The youngest (who asks the question) is now 13 years old (8+5).

P. 111 Nosing Around …

15.

P. 112 A Logical Sequence

X. The W is positioned 3 letters before the T, the T 4 letters before the P, the P 5 letters before the K, the K 6 letters before the E, and the E seven letters before X, if you count from A to Z.

P. 113 Counterbalance

Five orange balls.
One red is a blue plus an orange, so three red is three blue and three orange. Three blue is two green, so two green is two red plus two orange.
Three red is three orange plus two red plus three orange.
Remove two red from each side. What's left is one red equal to three orange which plus two orange is five orange.

P. 114 Puzzle 1

60. If 6 boys need 6 exercise books in 6 weeks, then 12 boys need 12 exercise books in 6 weeks, and 12 boys need 24 exercise books in 12 weeks.
If 4 girls need 4 exercise books in 4 weeks, then 12 girls need 12 exercise books in 4 weeks. So, 12 girls need 36 exercise books in 12 weeks.
In short: 12 girls and 12 boys need 24 + 36 (60) exercise books in 12 weeks.

P. 115 Puzzle 2

25. From top to bottom per bar the result is 53. You start by subtracting the numbers per bar, then adding them up per bar, subsequently subtracting and adding up.

P. 116 Puzzle 3
10. The letters represent their position in the alphabet.

P. 117 Puzzle 4
$3.

P. 118 Puzzle 5
The M. The letters represent their position in the alphabet. The sum of the letters at the far ends of the diagonals and the middle column and row, add up to 15, representing the O which stands in the middle.

P. 119 Puzzle 6
Michigan. Use the H in the next puzzle.

P. 120 Puzzle 7
The X. It is the only type of letter with a serif.

P. 121 Puzzle 8

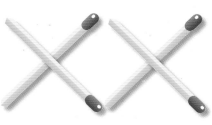

P. 122 The Exception
No. 2, the one that's mirrored.

P. 123 The Sentence
A natural death due to old age.

P. 124 From 8 to 10
Dollarized.

P. 125 Multi-Musical …
The notes of this piece can be played from top to bottom and bottom to top.

P. 126 Triangles!
12.

P. 127 Central Problem

The E. The letters represent their position in the alphabet. The letter in the first section minus the one from the third section is the letter in the middle. This applies to both diagonals and horizontally and vertically in the middle row and middle column.

P. 128 What's That For?

A pepper and salt pen. You can sprinkle salt or pepper by bending the pen at the top or the bottom.

P. 129 And What's Next?

The purple square skips two squares counterclockwise. The ball goes from square to square, also counterclockwise.

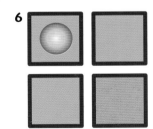

P. 130 LA Daytrip

Hollywood.

P. 131 Chess Puzzle

Liverpool.

P. 132 Logic!

22. There is a logical sequence if you start at 2, according to the direction of the text:
×2, -3, +4, and so on.

P. 133 Friday the Thirteenth …

There are 12 months in a year of (on average) 365 ¼ days. The 13th day of the month occurs once in 365 ¼ divided by 12. One week always has 7 days, so the Friday occurs

On average Friday occurs on the 13th day once every 213 days.

$$\frac{365¼ \times 7}{12} = \frac{2556¼}{12} = 213 \text{ days}$$

P. 134 I See, I See, What You See Too…

They are exactly the same color.

P. 135 Question From the Cross …

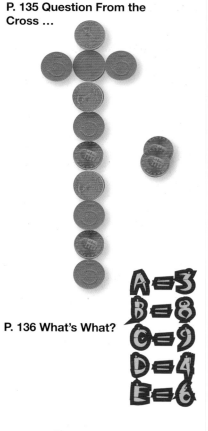

P. 136 What's What?

A = 3
B = 8
C = 9
D = 4
E = 6

P. 137 Math Genius …

19½ .

P. 138–139 Halfhearted 1, 2

A LA MAISON DE PARIS — 1, Rue Ricard, 1 — NIORT —

M. de Crac, en faisant boire son cheval après la bataille, s'aperçoit qu'il a été coupé en deux…
— Trouver l'autre moitié? —

A LA MAISON DE PARIS — 1, Rue Ricard, 1 — NIORT —

Il n'est pas de vraie sorcière sans corbeau?

P. 140 A Pattern

P. 141 Family Puzzle

26, including the husbands of the four daughters.

P. 142 A Birthday
Miriam was born just before midnight on February 28. Monique was born just after midnight on March 1. The year in the puzzle is a leap year, and February 29 falls in between the twins' birthdays.

P. 143 Next?
Each time a square changes into a circle, a triangle changes into a square, and a circle changes into a triangle.

P. 144 Strange Sum ...
4. Each following number consists of the result of the multiplication, of the digits of the number above it.

P. 145 Odd One Out ...
No. 3. It's the only one not forming a square with the bars.

P. 146 What's That For?
Chinese chopsticks for amateurs.

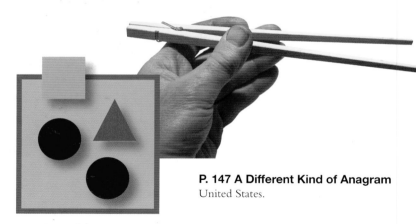

P. 147 A Different Kind of Anagram
United States.

P. 148 V, W, and X

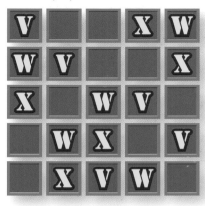

P. 149 Leading Anagrams

Charles de Gaulle
Julius Caesar
Abraham Lincoln
Richard Nixon
François Mitterand

P. 150 Lost Letters

F and H. The letters in their boxes refer
to their position in the alphabet. The
boxes connected by a line add up to 11.

P. 151 Far Away …

Seychelles.

P. 152 Broken Letters

P. 153 Where to Begin?

14 and 46. Follow the arrow in the
order of: +2, -8, ×2, +2, -8, ×2, etc.

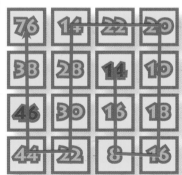

P. 154 Singing in the Rain …

He was bald.

P. 154-155 Cannon Fodder
A total of 55 cannonballs. The second layer contains 25 of them. The third layer 16, the fourth 9, the fifth 4 and 1 cannonball on top.

P. 156 Chess Puzzle
Sandcracks.

P. 157 Taxi!
If he was deaf, how could he have heard his passenger tell him the destination?

P. 158 One Cub Too Many ...
Six times. A tigress can't count, that's why she walks back once more. Then she discovers there are no more cubs.

P. 159 Self-Evident?
44. The sum of the digits the number consists of is added to the number to obtain the next number. 14 + (1 + 4) = 19, and so on.

P. 160 What's That For?
It's to help you pull up your shoelace.

P. 161 Famous Movie Stars
Clint Eastwood
Charles Bronson
John Wayne
Cary Grant
Bruce Willis

P. 162 Domino Sums ...
A double three set consists of the stones only containing the dots zero through three.

P. 163 A Bit of Calculating ...
$3333 \div 30 = 111.1$

P. 164 Domino Games

CONCORDE
TEJOBMUJ

P. 165 Divide and Rule...

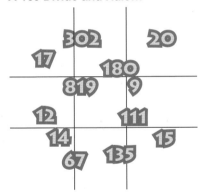

302   20
17
180
819   9
12   111
14   15
67   135

P. 167 Making the Connection ...

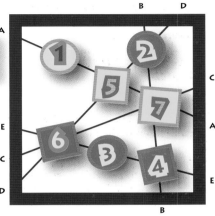

P. 168 A Drinking Problem
Take glass 4 and pour its contents into glass 1 and put glass 4 back where it was.

P. 169 Impolite ...
Do this puzzle with a friend. Ask her (or him) to write down her height in inches (centimeters). She then has to double the number and add five to it. The total is multiplied by 50, and to

the result of this 1756 is added. Of this number she has to subtract her year of birth and this is the number she has to tell you. The last two digits represent the age she has reached or will reach that same year.

P. 170 Fair and Square …
We were talking about a grandfather, his son and the son's son: three persons.

P. 171 Big, Bigger, Biggest …
The clowns are of the same size. Make a copy and cut it out. It appears as if they change in size depending on the order in which you lay them down. Try it with three or four pieces.

P. 172 In the Days of Yore
Greta Garbo
Simone Signoret
Audrey Hepburn
Marlene Dietrich
Mae West

P. 173 Soup Chicken?

P. 174 Next?
26. The difference between the two digits of the number is added to the number to obtain the next number. 14 + (4-1)=17, and so on.

P. 175 Turning This Way and That
Yes, it fits exactly in between, but the positions "below" and "to the side" help create an optical illusion. So, it's a question of measuring …

P. 176 Burning Problem

P. 177 Fitting Together Exactly

P. 178 What Is Missing?

5. The left and the right number are multiplied. The result is the number in the middle. From this the number on the right is subtracted. (4x5=20-5=15)

P. 179 Pears and Lemons, Anyone?

One lemon costs nine cents and a pear six cents.

P is pear and C is lemon.

In the puzzle it says:

$6P+9C=117$ (1) and $5P+11C=129$ (2).

By multiplying given (1) by 5 and given (2) by 6, you get $30P+45C=583$ (3) and $30P+66C=774$ (4).

Subtract (3) from (4) and you get: $66C-45C=774-585$, so $21C=189$, $C=189÷21=9$.

A lemon costs nine cents. Use the 9 for the lemon in the earlier equation and you get the price of a pear.

P. 180 Chimera?

10. In the direction of the arrow: $1+6=7$, $16+7=23$, $2+3=5$, $23+5=28$, and so forth.

P. 181 Brainy

3. For every row and column the sum of the first and third number is equal to the sum of the second and the fourth number.

P. 182 A Good Eye

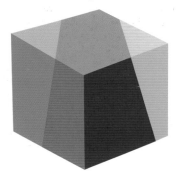

P. 183 Wedding Party

She worked at the Registry/County Clerk's office.

P. 184 Coin Puzzle

1. Move 7 under 8 and 9.
2. Move 8 on the inside against 4 and 6.
3. Move 1 downward to between 1 and 7.

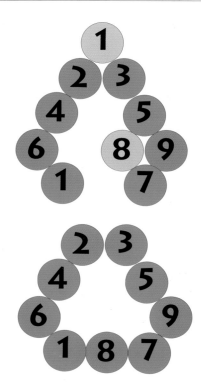

P. 185 Geometry

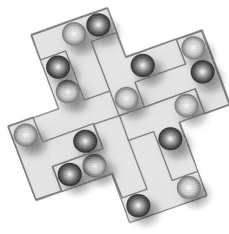

P. 186 Baseball
The bat costs $75 – the ball $50.

P. 187 Broken Letters

P. 188 What's That For?
A garlic peeler – you put the clove in the rubber holder and roll it back and forth between your hands.

P. 189 Hidden Letters
D and O. The letters in the boxes refer to their position in the alphabet. The boxes that are connected by a line add up to 15.

Index